TÉ

KNOW
THEGAME

Croquet

Produced in collaboration with
The Croquet Association

A&
CB

Produced for A & C Black by

Monkey Puzzle Media Ltd
The Rectory, Eyke, Woodbridge
Suffolk IP12 2QW

Published in 2008 by

A & C Black Publishers Ltd
38 Soho Square, London W1D 3HB
www.acblack.com

Fourth edition 2008

Note: While every effort has been made to ensure
that the content of this book is as technically accurate
and as sound as possible, neither the author nor the
publisher can accept responsibility for any injury or
loss sustained as a result of the use of this material.

This book is produced using paper that is made from
wood grown in managed, sustainable forests. It is
natural, renewable and recyclable. The logging and
manufacturing processes conform to the
environmental regulations of the country of origin.

Acknowledgements
Cover and inside design by James Winrow and
Tom Morris for Monkey Puzzle Media Ltd.
Cover photograph of Robert Fulford by Samir Patel.
Photographs by Quiller Barrett on pages 39, 50;
The Croquet Association on page 9; Dr Tim King on
pages 15, 18, 21, 22, 24, 27; Samir Patel on pages
14, 30; Grant Pritchard on pages 4, 8, 10–13, 17,
35, 36, 55; Ian Vincent on pages 29, 32, 41, 46, 53.
Illustrations by Dave Saunders.

Text by Ian Vincent, based on earlier editions by
Bill Lamb, John McCullough and Dr GL Ormerod.
Editorial consultant Quiller Barrett.

KNOW THE GAME is a registered trademark.

Printed and bound in China by C&C Offset Printing
Co., Ltd.

Note: Throughout the book players and officials are
referred to as 'he'. This should, of course, be taken
to mean 'he or she' where appropriate. Similarly, all
instructions are geared towards right-handed players
– left-handers should simply reverse these instructions.

CONTENTS

INTRODUCTION

Croquet can be played by people of all ages. It provides mental stimulation and physical exercise, and can be both highly competitive and a source of lasting friendships.

STRUCTURE OF THIS BOOK

The simplest description of croquet is that it is a game played on a grass court in which the players take it in turns to hit a ball with a mallet, to try to send balls through hoops. There are in fact several different games that can be played using the same equipment. This book describes the two that are widely played outside (and to some extent within) the USA: Golf Croquet and Association Croquet.

The first part of this book describes the court and equipment, and the basic action of hitting a ball with a mallet, which are common to both games. The other two parts describe Golf Croquet and Association Croquet respectively, each covering the strokes, tactics and laws that are specific to those games.

◀ Croquet can be played by men and women of all ages.

THE TWO GAMES

In Golf Croquet, each ball is played in sequence. All balls contest the same hoop, either trying to run it, get into position to do so, or to knock other balls away. The first ball to run a hoop scores the point for it and the balls then move on to the next hoop. The winner is the first to get an agreed number of points.

Association Croquet has been described as 'snooker on grass'. Extra strokes can be earned by running a hoop or hitting another ball with the ball you are striking. This means that a turn can last anywhere from one to ninety-one strokes. Each ball has to run all the hoops and hit the peg in the centre of the court. The winner is the first side to do this with both its balls.

WHERE TO PLAY

Croquet can be played on a modest sized lawn. The flatter and shorter the grass, the larger the court can be. However, to find out what the games really have to offer it is best to join a club. Clubs usually have better courts and equipment. They also have players who can show you the range of strokes and tactics that can be used, teach you the proper rules and provide wider competition. Most clubs welcome new members and offer coaching.

THE CROQUET ASSOCIATION

The Croquet Association is the governing body for croquet in England and Wales, which maintains a list of clubs on its website, http://www.croquet.org.uk, as well as a wealth of other information about the sport. The Association coordinates the national tournament calendar, and assists clubs and regional federations. Scotland, Ireland and a number of other countries have their own croquet associations and there is also a World Croquet Federation.

Golf and Association Croquet can both be enjoyed in a garden with a rectangle of reasonably level grass as small as 15 by 12 yards.

COURT AND EQUIPMENT

Most croquet clubs will provide all the equipment needed to play the game, as described below. Garden sets are also available if you have your own lawn. However, garden croquet equipment tends to be rather lightweight.

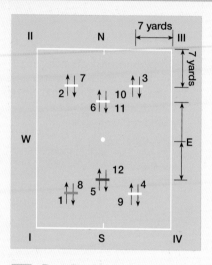

Fig. 1: The Golf Croquet court. The solid white line is the boundary.

Measurements for croquet are usually in imperial units (see table on pages 6–7 for metric

THE COURT

A full-size croquet court measures 35 x 28 yards and is bounded by a white line, the inside of which is the actual boundary. Smaller courts, laid out in the same proportion, are allowed and beginners are strongly advised to learn, practise and play on them, at least until they become proficient. The surface of the court should be flat and level, with the grass cut short enough to allow the balls to roll easily. About ½ inch is usually short enough, although for top class play the grass should be shorter.

The boundaries are named after the points of the compass for convenience when describing the game. This is quite arbitrary and bears no relation to the actual geographic orientation of the court. The corners of the court (I, II, III and IV) are named after the hoops (1, 2, 3 and 4) that lie nearest them.

Yard-lines

For Association Croquet, one yard inside the boundaries and running parallel to them are the yard-lines, but these are not marked out. The space between the boundary and the yard-line is known as the yard-line area. The points where the yard-lines intersect are called the corner spots and the small square enclosed by the yard-lines and the boundary lines at each corner is the corner square. There are two baulk-lines, where play starts, which run along the North and South yard-lines from corner III and corner I respectively to the centre of each yard-line.

METRIC CONVERSIONS

	Imperial	Metric
Standard court	35 yards	32.0 metres
	28 yards	25.6 metres
	7 yards	6.4 metres
	1 yard	0.9 metres
Peg	18 inches	450 millimetres
	6 inches	150 millimetres
	1½ inches	38 millimetres
Hoops	12 inches	300 millimetres
	3¾ inches	95 millimetres
Balls	3⅝ inches	92 millimetres
	16 ounces	454 grammes

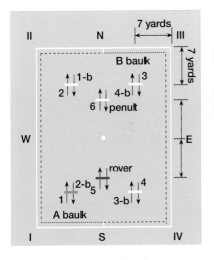

Fig. 2: The Association Croquet court. The solid white line is the boundary. The dashed black line is the yard-line. The area between the two is the yard-line area.

COURT SPEED

The speed of a court is measured by the time it takes for a ball hit from one end of the court to come to rest on the opposite boundary, 35 yards away. The longer the time, the faster the court (because the ball takes longer to slow down). Eleven seconds is a comfortable pace; less than 8 seconds requires the ball to be hit too hard for accuracy.

EQUIPMENT AND ACCESSORIES

A club will normally provide all equipment listed below, though experienced players may prefer to play with their own mallets.

- One peg, 1½ inch in diameter, 18 inch above the ground and painted white to a height of at least 6 inch above the ground, set in the centre of the court.

- Six hoops, with uprights 5/8 inch in diameter, 12 inch above the ground, painted white and allowing a gap between the uprights 1/8 inch larger than a ball. Hoop 1 has a blue top and hoop 5 (also the last hoop of the second circuit) has a red top. Hoops 1 to 4 are set 7 yards in from the boundary adjacent to their respective corners. Hoop 5 is 7 yards south of the peg and hoop 6 is 7 yards north of it. All hoops are set with their openings facing south-north.

- Four balls – blue, black, red and yellow (diameter 3⅝ inches, weight 1lb).

- Mallets, ideally one per player.

- Spring clips, to keep score.

- Blue, red, black and yellow flags in corners I–IV.

- White marker pegs.

- A check fence to halt the progress of balls sent off the court is useful.

Clothing

Flat-soled shoes, such as trainers, must be worn to avoid damaging the surface of the court. All other clothing is left to the choice of the individual, but whites are normally worn at tournaments and club matches. Clothing should allow the mallet to swing freely, so long skirts are best avoided. Rain does not stop play, so bring waterproofs. In sunshine, a hat and sun lotion are wise precautions.

 Loose-fitting trousers or shorts and top allow the mallet to swing freely.

A complete croquet set: **(1)** peg, **(2)** six hoops, **(3)** four balls, **(4)** four spring clips, **(5)** eight corner pegs, **(6)** four corner flags, **(7)** four mallets, **(8)** hoop hole maker and hammer.

MALLETS

Most mallets weigh roughly 3 lb. The head may be circular or rectangular in cross section and will be 9–12 inches long. The head is usually made of wood. The shaft may be wood (usually hickory or ash), metal, fibreglass or carbon fibre. The shaft is usually about 36 inches long, but this varies according to the height and grip of the player.

Before buying a mallet, try as many different weights and lengths as possible, to find one that suits you.

SINGLE-BALL STROKES

Although hitting a single ball with a mallet may look simple, various factors combine to produce a successful stroke. There is no single grip, style or stance that must be used. You need to find a combination that is comfortable for you and enables you to swing the mallet freely.

GRIPS

There are three main ways of gripping the mallet: the standard, Irish and Solomon grips. Each of the three grips is popular and there is no clear-cut advantage to any one of them. Beginners should adopt whichever grip feels most natural and comfortable. If the grip is not comfortable, repeated swinging of the mallet may lead to aching wrists or longer term injury.

Standard grip

The upper hand, usually the left hand for a right-handed player, grips the mallet with the fingers curled around the shaft and with the knuckles pointing forwards. The lower hand grips with the palm of the hand behind the shaft. It is usually better to have the hands close together, so that they share the work of swinging the mallet.

The standard grip. Some players find this rather unwieldy and prefer to keep the hands apart.

The Solomon grip. This grip allows a very free swing of the mallet

The Irish grip. A flexible top wrist is needed for this grip.

Irish grip

With the Irish grip both the upper and lower hands grip the shaft with the palms either behind or to the side. Some players like to extend the index finger of the upper hand along the shaft and to overlap this finger with the fingers of the lower hand. The grip is usually a little lower down the shaft of the mallet.

Players using the Irish grip often play with a shorter-shafted mallet, while those with a Solomon grip use a longer one.

Solomon grip

For this grip, both hands curl round the mallet shaft with the knuckles in front. The hands are usually together at the top of the mallet and some players have a longer than usual shaft.

JOHN SOLOMON

The Solomon grip is named after a famous player, John Solomon, who started with it as a small child and stayed with it as he grew. He won the Mens Championship in 1951, while still under 21, and a total of 48 championship titles in all. He was president of the Croquet Association from 1982 to 2004.

STYLE AND STANCE

Centre style

In the centre style the mallet is swung between the feet and legs while facing the target. The head is then naturally over the line of the swing. The feet should be placed parallel to the line of the swing and preferably side by side about 6-9 inches apart, so that the body is square to this line. The weight should be evenly distributed between the feet.

The swing is mainly from the shoulders, so the mallet and arms should feel as if they are swinging together. In this stance, bend forwards from the waist to allow the hands and arms enough room to move. Too upright a stance will inhibit this movement.

Golf style

Players requiring a lot of power for a stroke occasionally swing the mallet across the body (right to left for a right handed player) while facing perpendicular to the line of aim. However, this style is considered much less accurate and so is not normally used.

If you lose your balance when swinging the mallet, try a stance with one foot drawn back a little. Try not to draw back the hip and shoulder while doing this, as this will affect the line of the swing.

Centre style. Note that the body is bent to allow room for the hands to swing back.

Side style

In the side style the mallet is swung to the side of the feet and the body, while facing the target. The feet are usually placed with one foot in front of the other, with the weight mainly on the forward foot. The shoulders and hips should remain square to the line of aim. The grip for this style is usually the Standard grip, with the hands separated.

Side-style players often play with a longer-shafted mallet.

STALKING

Even if you are not aiming to hit another ball or run a hoop, it will pay to select a definite aiming point. Stand back from your ball along the extension of the line joining the aiming point and the ball. Walk forwards along this line, looking towards the aiming point, until you arrive at your ball and take up your stance. This method, known as 'stalking' the ball, will help to align your feet and body.

SWING

When you have taken up your stance, lower your mallet so that the mallet head is just behind the ball. Look up towards your target and then down again at the ball. Swing the mallet backwards by pulling with the arms – remember the swing comes from the shoulders – and then move it

steadily forwards, keeping your gaze fixed on the ball you are about to hit with the mallet. Hit the ball with the centre of the mallet face when the head is parallel to the ground and follow the swing through. Resist any temptation to look up too early to see where the ball has gone.

Practice makes perfect

The swing should be smooth and unhurried, particularly at the top of the backswing. Any jerkiness will spoil the accuracy of the hit. Practise hitting your ball so that it comes to rest on a spot on the court at a predetermined distance. Vary this distance so that you can hit accurately as far as the greatest distance you need. Don't try to hit harder on the more distant shots by forcing the forward swing; instead, lengthen the backswing and try to keep the same rhythm as for gentler strokes.

The follow through. Red runs the hoop thanks to a smooth follow-through.

FAULTS

There are a number of things you are not allowed to do when hitting the ball, which are called faults. To play a clean stroke, you must:

- hit the ball only once (except after making a roquet in Association Croquet)

- hit with the face (not the edge) of the mallet

- not 'crush' a ball against a hoop

- swing the mallet freely.

CASTING

Some players swing the mallet backwards and forwards over the top of the ball until they feel that the rhythm and direction of the swing are correct. Then they drop their hands or shoulders to strike the ball with a final forward swing. This is called casting.

The stroke is being refereed in case a fault is made.

HOOP RUNNING

The technique for playing your ball through the hoop (running the hoop) is that of a normal single-ball stroke. If the ball is directly in front of the hoop, stalk it carefully, aiming for a point in the centre of the hoop. Swing gently and smoothly, keeping your eye on the ball, and follow through normally.

Of course, more often than not, your hoop-running stroke will have to be made from an angle. Use the same technique, hitting only slightly harder. Aim so that the ball just misses the inside of the near wire and hits the far wire to carry on through the hoop.

When you are in a good position to run a hoop, you should try to use just enough force to make the ball stop where you want it to.

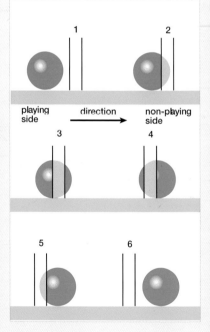

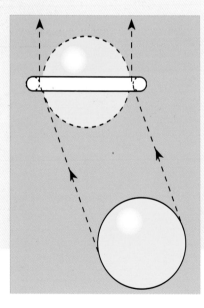

Fig. 3: Running an angled hoop: aim to miss the near wire.

Fig. 4: Balls in relation to a hoop: **1** and **2** have not started to run the hoop; **3** has started to run the hoop; **4** has not completed the running of the hoop; **5** and **6** have completed the running of the hoop.

JUMP STROKES

If you are faced with a very angled hoop, or there is another ball in the way, it may be possible to run the hoop by causing your ball to jump off the ground. To do this, stand further forward, hold the mallet further down the shaft and hit the ball while the mallet is still swinging downwards, taking care not to damage the court.

> **A smooth swing and follow-through will start the ball rolling and this forward spin will help it through the hoop.**

RUNNING A HOOP

A hoop is run when a ball goes through it in the required direction and comes to rest in a position where it cannot be touched by a straight edge placed against the front of the hoop (see Fig. 4).

A ball can take more than one stroke to run a hoop.

▶ A jump stroke. By hitting down on yellow, it jumped over red to run the hoop.

GOLF CROQUET

Golf Croquet is an interactive and tactical game. The balls are played in strict sequence, jockeying for position until one of them scores the hoop being contested. Scoring is like matchplay golf, hence the name.

OUTLINE OF THE GAME

Golf Croquet is played between two sides. The winner of the toss starts and plays with the blue and black balls. The other side plays with red and yellow balls. For doubles, each player strikes his own ball, but in singles a player strikes both balls of his side.

Getting started

The game starts by playing the balls in sequence from within a yard of corner IV, normally aiming to get in position to run hoop 1. Subsequent strokes are played from where the balls end up. If a ball crosses the boundary, it is placed where it crossed the line. Play continues until a ball scores the hoop, which

Blue will be played next, whether or not yellow runs the hoop. Its owner is on the court ready to play, but not in the striker's way.

it does by passing through it in the correct direction, south to north for hoop 1. Scoring a hoop gives its owner a point, but no extra stroke. The next ball in sequence is played from where it lies, but now contesting hoop 2.

CONTESTING A HOOP

Balls can contest a hoop by clearing or blocking opposing balls, or by promoting or protecting their partner ball. Even if one ball seems certain to run the hoop next time it is played, the other balls cannot directly play for position for the next one. If they are closer than half-way to the next hoop when a hoop is run they may be moved to one of the two penalty spots, which are peg high on either side of the court.

Order of hoops

The hoops are contested in the order 1 to 6 (clockwise round the outer four hoops, then from south to north up the centre of the lawn). Hoops 7 to 12 are hoops 2, 1, 4, 3, 6 and 5, but this time played in the other direction (anti-clockwise, then down the lawn, with the last hoop being played away from the peg). The game is won by the first side to get seven points; if the score is six-all after twelve hoops, hoop 3 is played again.

The score should be agreed after each hoop has been scored. In matches, a clip of the same colour as one of the balls belonging to the side that won it can be placed on the hoop to help keep count and for the benefit of any spectators.

The sequence of colours is shown on the centre peg: blue, red, black, yellow, then back to blue again.

GOLF CROQUET STROKE PLAY

Many strokes in Golf Croquet require you to hit your ball so that it hits another, either to knock it away (a clearance), or knock it into position (a promotion). On pages 10–17 we looked at how to hit a single ball into position and run a hoop. The technique for clearance and promotion strokes is essentially the same, though clearance strokes in particular tend to be hit hard, both to ensure that your ball travels straight and that the ball it hits is cleared a long way.

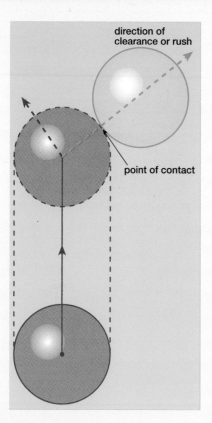

direction of clearance or rush

point of contact

CONTROLLING DIRECTION AND DISTANCE

There are two extra things to consider: the direction and distance the balls will go after one hits the other. These will be familiar to snooker or pool players.

If, for example, the ball you hit with your mallet (red) hits the target ball (blue) full on, then blue will go in the direction red was moving in and red will carry on in the same direction. The relative distance the two balls go depends on whether red is sliding or rolling when it hits blue. If it is sliding (as it will be if the balls are close together and red is hit hard), then, in a head-on collision, red will stop near to where blue was and blue will go as almost as far as red would have done had blue not been there. If, however, red

Fig. 5: Angled clearance or promotion stroke.

is rolling by the time it hits blue, red will carry on and blue will go less far. You can assist red to slide by hitting slightly up on it, or to roll by hitting slightly down.

If red hits the left-hand side of blue, blue will go to the right of the line of travel, and vice-versa. If you want blue to go along a particular line, you need red to hit it at the point where that line intersects the edge of blue (see Fig. 5). If it was sliding, red will be deflected along a line at right-angles; if rolling, it will tend to keep straighter.

If you find your ball is jumping after hitting the ball it is trying to clear, stand slightly further back to avoid hitting down on your ball.

Yellow attempts to clear blue to protect red.

GOLF CROQUET TACTICS AND LAWS

Golf Croquet tactics are generally fairly aggressive, because each hoop is almost a separate contest, so you don't give away too much if a shot goes badly wrong. However, there needs to be a balance between attack and defence.

GENERAL TACTICS

Each player is trying to gain position to run the hoop. Clearly, if a player's ball is in a good position in front of the hoop when the turn for that ball arrives, then the hoop should be run and so the point scored. However, the fact that the balls must be played in the correct sequence gives rise to interesting opportunities, according to the positions of all the balls on the court.

For conciseness in the following discussion, a colour without a capital letter refers to the ball and a colour with a capital refers to the player whose ball it is. For example, blue means the blue ball and Blue means the player of the blue ball.

Black could defend by knocking blue onto yellow to clear it, but the risk is that red will be left in position three turns later. Instead, he tried a jump shot to run the hoop.

1. Suppose Blue is to play and his ball is not in position to run the hoop but red is (see Fig. 6). Red is the next player in the sequence and there would be no point in Blue trying to improve the position of his own ball. Red would score the point before Blue's turn would come round again. Instead, Blue should play to remove red from its favourable position. Blue does this by aiming at red and striking blue firmly. Provided that the stroke is played accurately, blue will hit red and move it away. There are two advantages to playing the stroke as firmly as possible:

• the red ball will be moved as far as possible from the scene of action

• by striking blue firmly it will not pick up much rolling spin before the collision and, with a direct hit, will stay in position to run the hoop at its next turn.

Of course, if the stroke is not accurate and gives rise to a half-ball collision, blue will not stay in place but the main objective of removing red will have been achieved.

REPEATED CLEARANCES

Golf croquet often enters a phase where removing the opponent's next ball is most important and a spectacular series of hard-hit strokes results.

Remember that if there is a ball in a hoop you might be able to clear it from behind the hoop, or even get your ball to jump over it.

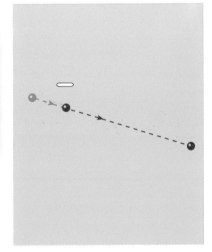

Fig. 6: Blue clears red, staying in position to run the hoop next time it plays.

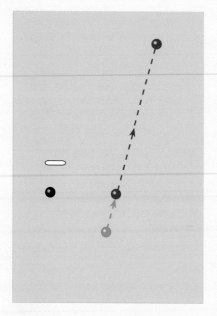

Fig. 7: Blue clears red to protect black.

2. Suppose blue is not in a position to run the hoop but the partner ball, black, is (see Fig. 7). Blue could play to take position also but that could result in a hard-hitting sequence as on page 23. It would be better for Blue to remove red as far as possible from the scene of action, preferably to a position where there is a hoop or ball between it and black.

3. Suppose in 2 (above) blue is not in a good position to remove red (see Fig. 8). The direct shot at red may be blocked by yellow. Now Blue can play to try to put his ball in position between red and black, so that Red in turn cannot remove black. It would be a mistake to try to play blue too close to black, as this may allow Red to remove blue and black in a single stroke. In fact, the closer that blue can be played to the red, the greater the chance of success, as blue will cut off a greater angle for red.

With yellow nowhere in sight, and both blue and black in position, red tries to jump over them to score the hoop.

WRONG BALL

It is surprisingly easy to get confused about which ball should play next. If (in singles) you play your partner ball (e.g. yellow instead of red) and the error is noticed immediately, you put the balls back and play the correct one. However if you play an opponent's ball, or (in doubles) your partner's ball, or any ball when not your turn to play, your opponent decides whether the balls are replaced and which ball to play next.

4. Suppose Blue is to play and no ball is in position to run the hoop (see Fig. 9). It may be possible to promote black into a hoop-running position with blue. Ambitious players may even try to get both balls in position with a half-ball collision.

> Other more advanced tactics are available, depending on the quality of the court and the accuracy of the players.

Fig. 8: Blue blocks red from clearing black, as yellow prevents blue clearing red.

Fig. 9: Blue promotes black into position to run the hoop when it plays.

HANDICAP PLAY

Handicap system

If you start playing at a club you will be given a handicap. Someone better than you will have a lower handicap and will give you the same number of extra turns as the difference in your handicaps. An extra turn entitles you to an extra stroke with the ball you just played, with which you can do anything except score a point.

Extra turns can also be used defensively, to stop the opponent scoring, but unless you are scoring points they will quickly run out.

Using extra turns

Extra turns are best used to enable you to score a point next time your side plays. For example, if you have just run hoop 3 fairly hard, but have not ended up in front of hoop 4, you could take an extra turn to get into a good position for hoop 4, while the other balls are still too far away to have much chance of clearing you. Similarly, if blue is to play with black in good position for a hoop, but red is nearby and blue is too far away, or obstructed from clearing it, you could play (see Fig. 10) to get blue in position to clear red and then use an extra turn to clear it.

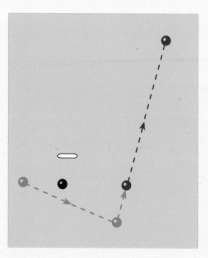

Fig. 10: Blue needs an extra turn to clear red in order to protect black.

LAWS

The definitive laws are on the CA web site: http://www.croquet.org.uk. Here is a summary of them.

1. The opposing sides are blue and black against red and yellow; doubles or singles can be played.

2. Each side plays alternately and a turn consists of a single stroke.

3. The balls are played in strict sequence: blue, red, black and yellow.

4. The side whose ball first runs the hoop scores the point (even if it was not the ball played in that turn). Then all balls go on to contest the next hoop.

5. The winner is the first side to score seven points.

6. The peg remains in place but is not used to score a point. If the sides are level after the last hoop, hoop 3 is contested again to decide the winner.

7. The game starts by playing the balls in sequence, starting with blue, from any point within one yard of corner IV.

8. A player may play a ball towards the hoop following the one being contested, but no further than the half-way line that is equidistant from the two hoops, unless it hit an opponent's ball first. If this rule is breached, the ball is moved to one of the penalty spots.

9. A ball that leaves the court is replaced on the boundary where it crossed the inside of the line.

EGYPTIANS DOMINATE

At the start of 2008, both the Men's and Women's World Golf Croquet Champions were from Egypt. Egyptian players typically hit the ball very hard, with a double jointed action, resulting in long and accurate clearances and hoop strokes.

This Egyptian player jumped yellow cleanly over black, but if it had caught it so that both balls ran the hoop in that stroke, black would score it as it was closer to the hoop.

ASSOCIATION CROQUET

Association Croquet is played between two sides and can take the form of singles or doubles. Each side has two balls – blue and black always play together on one side against red and yellow. In singles, each player has two balls. In traditional doubles, each player has his own ball but it is possible to play alternate stroke doubles, in which the partners take alternate strokes with whichever ball their side is playing.

OUTLINE OF THE GAME

The object of the game is for a side to get both its balls through each of the hoops in the prescribed order and then to hit the peg, before the other side completes the course. A point is scored for each hoop run and for hitting the peg. A full game requires 26 points for the winning side – 12 hoop points (1 to 6, 1-back to 4-back, penult and rover as shown in the diagram on page 7) and one peg point for each ball, but shorter games can be played.

SEQUENCE OF PLAY

The sides play alternate turns, choosing at the start of each turn which of their balls they will play with. A turn consists of one or more strokes, played by hitting that ball – the striker's ball – with a mallet.

In the first four turns, the balls are played into the game from anywhere along either baulk-line.

The striker is entitled to play one stroke at the start of a turn, but can earn extra strokes by making his ball hit one of the others (a 'roquet') or run. Running its hoop earns one continuation stroke, played from where the striker's ball ended up.

A STRATEGIC GAME

Association Croquet is a strategic game that has a stroke named after it. A 'croquet stroke' is played by hitting a ball after placing it in contact with another one, so that both balls move.

In this doubles game, the striker is attempting a long hoop 1, in the hope of starting a break. His opponents sit waiting for their turn to play.

Taking croquet

A roquet earns two extra strokes. Before the first of them, the striker takes croquet by picking up his ball and placing it in contact with the ball it roqueted, where that ball ended up. He then hits the striker's ball with his mallet, so that both balls move. The second extra stroke is a continuation stroke, played from where the striker's ball went in the croquet stroke. However, the turn ends without a continuation stroke if the croqueted ball is sent off the court, or the striker's ball goes off without running its hoop or making a roquet.

Once croquet has been taken from a ball, it becomes dead and croquet cannot be taken from it again until the striker's ball has run its hoop, or a new turn starts. By earning extra strokes in this way, a skilful player can run several, or even all, the hoops for the striker's ball in a single turn, known as making a break.

Alternate stroke doubles keeps both players more involved and is good for coaching.

ASSOCIATION CROQUET STROKE PLAY

By learning how to rush a ball, you will be able to control where the subsequent croquet stroke is played from. Mastering croquet strokes will enable you to send both balls to useful positions on the court.

HITTING IN

At the start of a turn, your ball may be a long way from any of the other balls and so you are just aiming to hit one of them. This will allow you to continue the turn and so you are not worried where the ball ends up. This is called hitting in. To hit in, stalk the ball and use your normal swing, but hit fairly hard, so that any slopes on the lawn have less effect.

Black is rushing red towards hoop 1 (which is out of shot to the bottom left of the picture). Black will then take croquet from red there.

RUSHING

If the balls are close together, say a yard or less, you have some control over where the roqueted ball will go and where you will play the croquet stroke from. This is called a rush (an angled rush is called a cut-rush). The technique for rushing a ball is the same as that for a clearance or promotion stroke in Golf Croquet (see pages 20–21), except that it doesn't matter where the striker's ball ends up, as you are going to pick it up. It is not a fault if you hit it again with your mallet after making a roquet.

You should be aiming to rush a ball to where you want to play the next croquet stroke from. The better your rush, the easier your next stroke will be. To prevent your ball jumping, avoid hitting down on it.

CROQUET STROKES

Once you have made a roquet your ball becomes 'in hand'. You pick it up and place it anywhere you wish in contact with the ball you have just roqueted. You then take croquet from that ball by striking your own ball with the mallet, so that both balls go where you want. There are many different ways of playing croquet strokes, depending on the distances and directions that you want the two balls to go.

Straight croquet strokes

These strokes are played so that the mallet is swung along the line joining the centres of the two balls in contact and thus passing through their point of contact. In this case both balls will travel along this line and the only problem is to get each ball to travel the correct distance. The harder you hit your ball the

further the two balls will go for a given style of stroke. You can change the ratio of the distances the two balls travel by altering your grip, stance and swing.

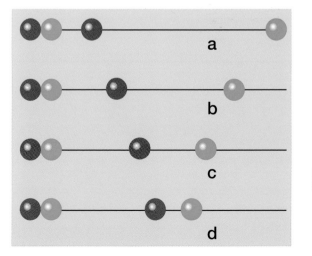

Fig 11: Typical ratios for
(a) the stop shot;
(b) the drive;
(c) the half-roll;
(d) the full roll.

Drives

The drive is hit in exactly the same way that you would hit a single ball shot, with the head of the mallet level at impact and with a normal follow-through. Naturally, you will feel more resistance at impact, because you are moving two balls rather than one. Apart from the take-off (see page 37), this is by far the easiest croquet stroke, because you are not trying to do anything special.

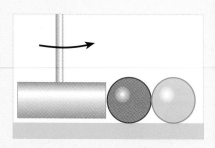

Fig. 12: The mallet is level with normal follow-through.

The heel of the mallet has been grounded just after playing a stop shot. Note that the player is standing back with his hands at the top of the shaft.

The croqueted ball will travel three to four times as far as your ball, irrespective of how hard you hit it. The actual ratio achieved depends upon the weight of your mallet, the stiffness of its shaft and the normal position of your hands.

Stop shots

Stop shots are the strokes to play when you want to increase the relative distances the two balls travel, sending the croqueted ball much further than your own. The shot is played most easily with a relaxed grip, with the hands well towards the top of the shaft and without a follow-through.

Many players stand back a little when addressing the ball for a stop shot, thus slightly raising the front face (toe) of the mallet head. On the forward swing the rear face (heel) of the mallet is grounded by pushing the mallet downwards on impact in order to prevent a follow-through. This is a very effective technique, but it does require good timing. The swing should remain smooth and care should be taken not to jab the mallet forwards.

MASTERING THE STOP SHOT

Once you have mastered the action of the stop shot you should be able to send the croqueted ball easily six times as far as your own ball. Good players can get ratios as high as 10:1. If you cannot get a good stop shot ratio, it may be that your mallet is too heavy.

It is worth pacing out the two distances to calculate your drive ratio when you first practise the stroke, as it will help in future shot selection.

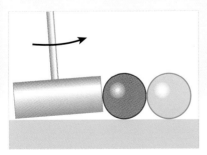

Fig. 13: The stop shot. The mallet is on the upswing, with minimum follow-through.

Rolls

Roll strokes are the opposite of stop shots. Use them when you want to send your own ball further in relation to the croqueted ball. Lower your grip with both hands and stand closer to the ball. You will have to bend much more from the waist and at the knee to address the ball. It is difficult to maintain your balance in this position if your feet are side by side, so your right foot (for a right-handed player) should be withdrawn. Your weight should be mostly on your front foot, which should be parallel to the line of swing.

In this position you will be addressing the ball with the heel of the mallet raised and hitting your ball on the downward swing before the mallet head becomes horizontal. Whilst some follow-through is acceptable, be careful not to make this excessive. Pushing the back ball after the croqueted ball has moved is a fault, as is striking it twice in the same stroke.

INFINITE VARIETY

Although only three types of straight croquet strokes have been described, there is an infinite graduation from an extreme stop shot through to a pass roll (one in which the striker's ball overtakes the croqueted ball"). Once you add the possibility of sending the balls apart at an angle, it is possible to send the two balls to precise positions over quite a large area of the court. However, it is impossible to split them apart by more than 90 degrees.

Black is about to be sent the same distance as red in this roll stroke.

Fig. 14: The roll. The mallet hits down with maximum follow-through.

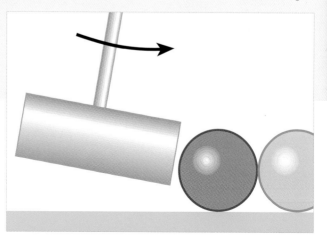

2. Determine where you want the two balls to end up.

3. Aim your swing at an imaginary point half-way between those positions.

4. Choose the kind of stroke to play (stop shot, drive or roll), depending on the relative distances you want the two balls to go.

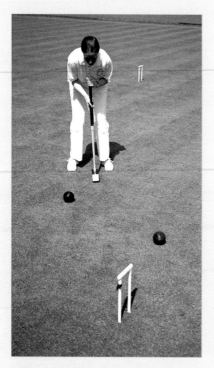

In this split croquet stroke, black is going toward the front of the hoop and red behind.

Split croquet strokes

The croquet strokes described so far have all been in a straight line. In a split croquet stroke, the two balls are sent in different directions. The ability to play a precise split shot is one of the hallmarks of a good player. To do so:

1. Place your ball behind and in contact with the roqueted ball, so that the line joining the centres of the two balls is in the direction you want the roqueted ball to go.

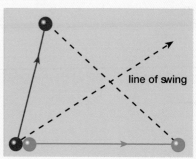

line of swing

Fig. 15: In a split croquet stroke, the striker should aim at the mid-point of the line between the intended position of the balls. Blue goes off along the line of centres.

The wider the angle of split, the further the striker's ball will go relative to the croqueted ball for a given kind of stroke.

Take-offs

A take-off is almost like a single-ball shot, in that only one ball moves any distance. It is used when you want to send your own ball to some other spot, leaving the croqueted ball almost where it lies.

To do this, place your own ball in contact with the roqueted ball so that their line of centres is at right angles to the direction in which you want your ball to go. Rather than hitting your ball precisely in that direction, you need to aim slightly to the side that the roqueted ball is on, to ensure that it moves when you hit your ball.

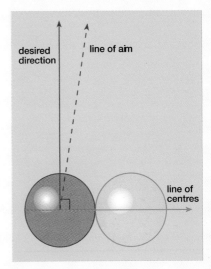

Fig. 16: A take-off is the easiest of the croquet strokes to play.

It is useful to develop a good touch on this shot. A good take-off to a ball twenty yards away may leave you with a simple one-yard roquet or a useful rush. A poor one may leave an awkward five-yarder.

AVOIDING A FAULT

It is a fault not to move or shake the croqueted ball, or to hit it with your mallet. While expert players can play this stroke so that the croqueted ball merely shakes, it is far safer for beginners to aim to move the croqueted ball about one inch for every yard that their own ball travels.

HOOP APPROACHES

Hoop approaches are the croquet strokes you play to get your ball into position to go through the hoop in the next stroke. However, this is not the only objective of a hoop approach. After you have run the hoop with your ball, you will usually want to rush the ball you approached the hoop with to get a better position for the next croquet stroke, so it is important to position the croqueted ball accurately as well. It is easier to get a good position to run a hoop if the hoop approach is made from a position reasonably close to it. Hoop approaches are classified by the positions from which they are made.

Front or normal approach
This approach is made from a position in front of the hoop. Before making the hoop approach, think what you want to do next.

If you want to go straight ahead, for example after hoops 1 or 3, you should send the croqueted ball well past the hoop with a stop shot.

If you want to go sideways, for example after hoops 2 or 2-back, you should send the croqueted ball only a little ahead and to the appropriate side with a half-roll.

If you want to reverse direction, for example after hoops 4 or 4-back, send the roqueted ball to the appropriate side and just past the hoop with a three-quarter roll.

Side approach
If in your previous stroke you have rushed the roqueted ball to the side of the hoop, you will have to play a little split stroke to croquet that ball behind the hoop and to leave your ball in a position to run it. Be careful here to aim correctly and swing along that line.

Backward approach
If you rushed the roqueted ball behind the hoop, you will have to approach the hoop with a take-off, (in this case called a backward take-off). Place your ball in contact with the roqueted ball on the side away from the hoop, so that it will stop at a suitable point in front of the hoop, and swing towards near wire of the hoop.

SIDE APPROACH PITFALLS

There is always a strong temptation to allow the swing to wander in the direction you want your ball to go; this inevitably results in your ball being too far from the hoop. Always allow a reasonable margin of error on this shot. If you attempt to get too close to the hoop with your ball, you have to be very accurate.

Blue is just about to approach hoop 1 by taking croquet from red, which will be sent 2–3 yards behind the hoop, so that blue will have a rush towards hoop 2 after running hoop 1.

Getting a rush after running a hoop may make all the difference to whether you can run the next hoop in that turn.

ASSOCIATION CROQUET BREAKS

Throughout the game your aim should be to 'make a break' – to score more than one point in a single turn. Everyone's ambition is to reach the stage of proficiency when they can take a ball round the course from the first hoop to the last in a single turn – an all-round break. Expert players can not only do this, but can also peel (push) their partner ball through several of its hoops in the same turn.

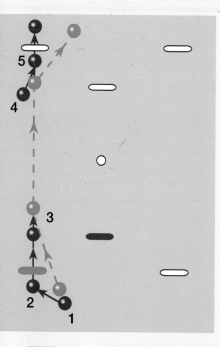

TYPES OF BREAK

Breaks are classified according to the number of balls used in making them. There are three kinds: two-ball, three-ball and four-ball. The more balls used in a break, the more difficult it is to arrange but the easier to sustain once set up.

TWO-BALL BREAK

With a two-ball break you have only one other ball to help you. This break is naturally the easiest to pick up, as you have a potential two-ball break whenever you are in a position to rush a ball to your next hoop. However, to keep the break going requires a good deal of skill (or luck).

Fig. 17: **1** Red approaches hoop 1 off blue, sending blue well behind the hoop.
2 Red runs the hoop with control.
3 Red rushes blue towards hoop 2.
4 Red approaches hoop 2, sending blue behind and to the right.
5 Red runs hoop 2 under control, with a rush to hoop 3.

Suppose you have to run hoop 1 with your ball and have rushed a ball to it (see Fig. 17). In the hoop approach, you must send the croqueted ball past the hoop to a position where it may be subsequently rushed to hoop 2. After playing the approach, you must run the hoop carefully with the right strength to obtain the rush. You must then rush the ball to hoop 2 accurately over a distance of about 20 yards.

THE ONE-BALL GAME

An enjoyable practice, or even serious, game is to play with each side having only one ball. In this game, a two-ball break is the only one that can be played and a break of even a few hoops can make all the difference to the outcome.

There are three strokes in the sequence for each subsequent hoop:

1. the hoop approach

2. the hoop-running stroke

3. the rush to the next hoop.

All three strokes must be performed accurately in order to get position at the next hoop.

Yellow approaches hoop 2, putting black behind and to the striker's right, to give a rush to hoop 3 after running the hoop.

THREE-BALL BREAK

With the three-ball break there are two other balls to help you. One ball, the pilot, is handily placed by the next hoop in order; the other, the pioneer, is waiting at the next hoop but one. The pilot is there to help you negotiate the next hoop and make a roquet (ideally a rush) afterwards (see diagram). It is then sent to act as a pioneer a hoop ahead of the break, whilst your ball finishes close to the pilot (previously the pioneer) at the next hoop.

There are five strokes in the sequence for each subsequent hoop (see Fig. 18):

1. the hoop approach

2. the hoop-running stroke

3. the roquet or rush on the pilot

4. the croquet stroke sending the pilot to be a pioneer at the next hoop but one.

5. the roquet on the pilot for the next hoop.

MAINTAINING ACCURACY

To sustain the break, the pioneers must be sent out accurately at stroke four of the sequence. The roquet or rush on the previous pilot at stroke three should be to a position which makes stroke four as easy as possible. To get a good rush at stroke three, each preceding stroke must also be accurate.

Fig. 18: Three-ball break. Red is the ball starting a break at hoop 1, blue the pilot for hoop 1, black the pioneer for hoop 2 (also true of Fig. 19).

When control of the break is lost, the succeeding strokes become more difficult. If the pilot can only be roqueted where it is, a split croquet stroke has to be played instead of a simple straight one.

FOUR-BALL BREAK

With this break (see Fig. 19) there are three other balls to help you. As with the three-ball break, there is a pilot at the next hoop and a pioneer at the next hoop but one. The extra ball is called the pivot, and is usually located somewhere in the vicinity of the peg. The presence of the pivot eliminates some of the most difficult strokes, although it increases the number of strokes in the sequence to seven. The strokes are as follows:

1. the hoop approach

2. the hoop-running stroke

3. the roquet or rush on the pilot

4. the croquet stroke sending the pilot to be a pioneer at the next hoop but one; the player's ball finishes close to the pivot

5. the roquet on the pivot

6. the croquet stroke (usually a take-off) to send the player's ball to the pilot at the next hoop

7. the roquet on the pilot for the next hoop.

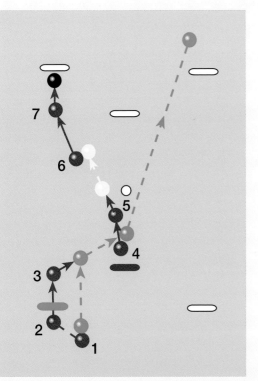

Fig. 19: Four-ball break. The roles of red, blue and black are as in Fig. 18 – yellow in this figure is the pivot ball.

Upgrading a break

Because a four-ball break is easier to play, you should try to upgrade any other break by bringing extra balls into it. A two-ball break may be upgraded to a three-ball break, if there is another ball that could be rushed to your next hoop, by rushing the pilot towards it after making a hoop. The next croquet stroke puts the old pilot as a pioneer at the next hoop but one, leaving a rush on the third ball to the next hoop (see Fig. 20 below).

During a three-ball break the fourth ball is easiest to pick up from a corner or a boundary as play approaches the hoop nearest to it. Fig. 21 shows the continuation of the previous position with yellow in corner III. After hoop 2 black is rushed further in court to become the pivot and red takes off to and roquets yellow. In the following croquet stroke yellow is sent as a pioneer to hoop 4, with red finishing close to the pilot, blue, at hoop 3.

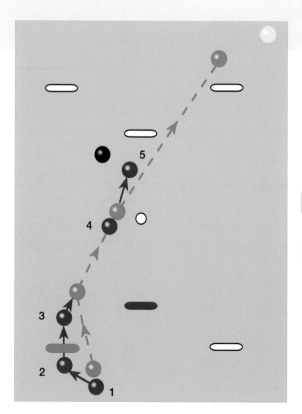

Fig. 20: Two-ball to three-ball break. Black is brought into play before hoop 2; yellow is of no use at this stage.

Advantages to the four-ball break

There are several advantages to the four-ball break in comparison with the two-ball and three-ball breaks:

- all the strokes are relatively short and straight, and consequently easier

- it does not matter so much if you don't get a rush on the pilot after making a hoop

- if you don't succeed in getting a good pioneer at stroke four, there is still a chance to send the pivot to act as the pioneer.

> **To avoid long croquet strokes, try to keep your pioneers inside the rectangle formed by the four outer hoops.**

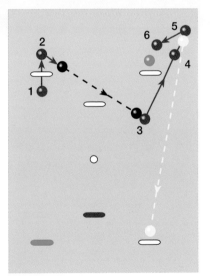

Fig. 21: Three-ball to four-ball break. After running hoop 2, the pilot, black, is rushed to the middle of the lawn to become the pivot. Red takes off to yellow, sends it as a pioneer to hoop 4, and makes hoop 3 off blue.

KEEPING A BREAK GOING

It is possible to vary the standard pattern for a break to suit the conditions and your own shot preferences. Some players like to rush long distances, others to play long croquet strokes. You can also look for opportunities to put out a pioneer two hoops in advance, e.g. for 2-back after making hoop 5, while the distances are shorter.

ASSOCIATION CROQUET TACTICS

At the start of the game a coin is tossed, traditionally by the better player. The winner of the toss can choose either to start or play second, or to have either pair of balls. The loser has the remaining choice. With experienced players there is no real advantage to be gained by choosing to play first. With weaker players it may be slightly better to do so (see pages 56–57 for handicap play).

OBJECTIVE IN THE OPENING

The first two turns of each side are used to play the four balls on to the court. Each ball may be played from any point on either baulk-line at the striker's choosing.

There is little point in trying to run the first hoop from A baulk. If you make the hoop, you merely score one point with little opportunity to continue with a break. If you fail and bounce back off the wire, you present your opponent with a chance to make an easy roquet and maybe a break. The start of the game is really a contest to gain the innings and take control of the game. Most games start with the standard opening, as follows.

▶ Having won the toss, Great Britain decided to play first; the New Zealand pair chose blue and black.

- If Bab hits the tice, she plays a take-off to K, moving R further up the court – at least to half-way. She then roquets K and lays a rush towards R. It is unlikely that Ray will hit in on the fourth turn as there is no easy shot. Bab would then continue with the rush to R, croquet K towards hoop 2 and leave a rush on R to hoop 1.

- If Bab declines to shoot at the tice, she should join up with K on the east boundary.

STANDARD OPENING

Let's suppose that Bab has won the toss and chosen to play first. Ray has chosen to play with R and Y.

1. Bab plays a ball, say K, from A baulk off the court on the east boundary in the vicinity of hoop 4.

2. Ray lays a 'tice' with R (he or she plays it from A baulk to a point on the west boundary a few yards from corner 1). Ray does this to entice Bab to shoot at it and miss. The length of the tice will depend upon Ray's estimate of Bab's prowess in shooting: too long and Bab will ignore the tice; too short and Bab will probably hit.

3. Bab must now assess the position. If she thinks she can hit the tice or that Ray will probably do so, she should shoot at the tice from corner one. This should be played sufficiently firmly so that B will finish in or near corner II if the tice is missed.

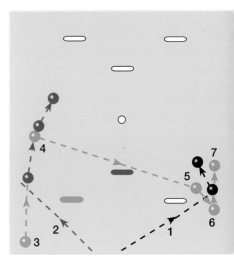

Fig. 22: The Opening: Bab hits the tice (red) with blue, at the start of the third turn, and then takes off to lay-up with its partner ball, black.

4. Ray must now play Y on to the court. Ray's options will be determined by Bab's play at turn 3.

• If Bab has hit the tice or declined it, Ray should shoot at R from a position on A baulk. This will leave Y in or near corner II, should he miss. If he hits, he should take off with Y to the joined up K and B, roquet one, and croquet it out a little into court, leaving a rush to hoop 1 on the other.

• If Bab has played at the tice and missed, Ray should shoot at it at an angle from A baulk. This will ensure that R and Y are joined up if he misses.

Of these possibilities the advantage goes to Bab if:

• she shoots at the tice and hits; or

• she ignores the tice and Ray misses it (see Fig. 23).

The advantage goes to Ray if:

• Bab misses the tice (see Fig. 24); or

• she ignores the tice and he hits it.

The standard opening is thus nicely balanced. Each player has the opportunity to gain the advantage with a good shot or hoping that the opponent misses.

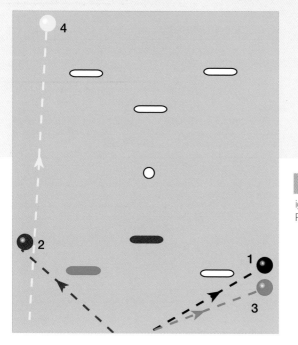

Fig. 23: The opening: Bab ignores the tice; Ray misses.

MID-GAME TACTICS

Like many sports, there is a range of tactical choices to be made in croquet, some attacking (like taking on a long red in snooker), and some defensive (like safety play). While it is your turn, your opponent can do nothing to affect your play, but where you leave the balls at the end of your turn will have a considerable impact on him.

IN-PLAYER TACTICS

In croquet the advantage lies with the player who has the innings; the player who has hit a roquet and is playing a turn of more than one stroke. He is known as the 'in-player', and has the chance of making a break. However, if you are the in-player, you must also try to retain that advantage at the end of your turn. However, there is more to it than just separating the opponent's balls and re-joining your partner ball. You should actually try to construct a leave that will allow you to make progress on your next turn, whatever your opponent does – provided, of course, that he does not hit in and so wrest the advantage from you.

By the end of your turn your balls should be close together and your opponent's should be well separated both from each other and yours. This is known as 'laying up' or 'making a leave'.

Fig. 24: The opening: Bab misses the tice; Ray misses the shot.

Taking risks

You should be aware, when playing your turn, of your capability with the various strokes employed. Sometimes it will be necessary at the start of a turn to play one or two difficult shots in order to pick up a break. This may entail some danger of breaking down and conceding the innings to your opponent. You have to weigh up the reward that will come from success against the penalty that will ensue from failure.

If the odds are against you, then it is time to play safe: use your turn to rearrange the balls on the court to your advantage with a view to making progress on your next turn.

Instead of risking the long angled hoop 2, Ray is about to play red to a position about a yard NW of yellow in the last stroke of his turn. Blue is by hoop 3 and black out of shot by hoop 1. Red is for hoop 2; blue for 3 and both black and yellow for 1. This is a very strong leave, as whichever ball Bab plays, Ray will have at least a 3-ball break for one of his balls next turn (unless Bab hits in). If Bab shoots at red or yellow, Ray will be able to start his turn by roqueting it where it will be placed on the yard-line.

OUT-PLAYER TACTICS

The out-player is the player who does not have the innings. When it is your turn to play, you will be faced with two immediate decisions: which ball to play with and what to do with it.

Which ball?

- If your opponent has broken down and left one of your balls close to one of his, then obviously play with it.

- If your opponent has made a good leave, play with the ball that is by your opponent's next hoop unless you have a very good chance of hitting in with the other ball. If your opponent has left each of your balls by one of his hoops, play with the one that is by the hoop of his backward ball.

- If your opponent has not made a good leave and you have a free choice of ball to play with, play with the ball that will give you the best chance to make a break if you hit in.

What to do?

- If your opponent has broken down with his balls widely separated and you have no easy roquet, join up with your partner ball.

- If you have a free shot at any ball (one that will leave your ball in a safe position) take that shot.

- If a free shot is not available, assess the danger of shooting at and missing one of the other balls in comparison with your chance of hitting in and making a break. The danger will depend upon your opponent's skill as well as your own. If the odds seem in your favour, take the shot.

- If the odds above seem too unfavourable, play your ball to a safe position and wait for a better opportunity. The safe position will usually be in or close to a corner behind the break of your opponent's preferred ball. For example, if your opponent's backward ball is for hoop 4, then play to the third corner.

AUNT EMMAS

Risk management is an important part of the tactics of croquet, but don't take it too far. Avoid becoming the type of player who doesn't try to make a break and does nothing but separate the opponent balls on each turn. Such players are known as 'Aunt Emmas', and are deservedly unpopular and rarely successful.

END-GAME TACTICS

Once a ball has run all its hoops, it becomes a 'rover' and can score the peg point by hitting the peg, (pegging out). It is then removed from the court and plays no further part in the game. A rover ball may also peg out any other rover ball by causing it to hit the peg. This means that special tactics are needed towards the end of a game.

Pegging-out

The ideal is to rush your partner ball close to the peg, peg it out in the croquet stroke and then peg out your own ball with the continuation stroke. (Be careful not to rush it on to the peg, as your turn ends if you have nothing to take croquet from.)

Line the balls up carefully (see Fig. 25) so that the line through their centres points to the centre of the peg. It is best to check this from near ground level, either looking over the top or along each side of the balls. Make certain that the two balls are in contact and play a firm, straight drive, so that your ball will finish a couple of feet past the peg if it does not hit it.

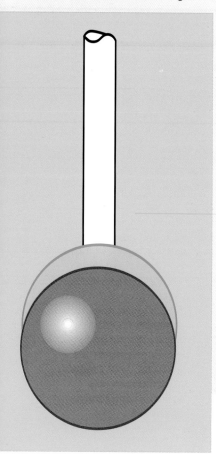

If you are too far from the peg to be confident of pegging out the croqueted ball, either roll both balls near the peg and peg out the striker's ball, or just leave a rush to the peg so that you can peg out next turn.

Fig. 25: Lining up the peg out

Arranging for the peg out

If your forward ball is for the peg and you are playing a break with your backward ball, you should finish in that turn. Try to arrange the break so that your partner ball is not the pioneer at rover, so that you can leave it by the peg.

However, it is not wise to run the rover hoop with your forward ball while your other ball is a long way behind (except possibly in a handicap game). You run the risk of having your ball pegged out by your opponent, leaving you without a partner ball to join up with at the end of your turns. Where you should stop with your forward ball depends on the state and standard of play: good players will be able to 'peel' another ball through one or more hoops and peg it out in a single turn.

▼ Having played a break with yellow, the striker is about to peg out red and yellow from close range to win the game.

Rover peel

If you have just one hoop left to run with your forward ball, you may be able to peel it through with the backward ball and peg both balls out to finish the game.

Arrange the break so that your partner ball is the pioneer at rover. Take one of the opponent's balls up to rover after making penult (the last hoop but one) and croquet it just past and to one side of rover. Roquet or rush your partner ball in front of rover and peel it through firmly with the croquet stroke. Run rover gently with your own ball and roquet the opponent's ball. Take off to get position behind your partner ball and rush it to the peg to peg out.

Three-ball endings

If you have pegged out one of your opponents balls, you should try to avoid leaving him a shot at either of your balls, unless you can pick up a three-ball break if he misses. Provided you have not touched his ball since he last played it, you can leave your balls wired from his without conceding a lift. If your backward ball is well ahead of your opponent's ball, you could peg out your forward ball to leave a two-ball ending.

If you are the player with the single ball, you should generally try to hit-in at every opportunity, unless you will be leaving an easy break if you miss. If there is no safe shot, play your ball off the court near to your opponent's next hoop, or between his balls if he has not joined up.

Two-ball endings

If one ball from each side has been pegged-out, neither side can have the innings as they do not have a partner ball to join up with. All you can do is run your hoop if you are in front of it, try and roquet your opponent's ball (either to make a two-ball break or to reposition the balls to your advantage), or play for position to do one of these next turn. If neither side tries to roquet the other's ball, the game can turn into a procession, but it is often an advantage to be a hoop behind.

> **Don't take risks in trying the peel; it is far better to end the turn with a tidy leave for peg and rover than to break down with several balls around the rover hoop.**

Fig. 26: The peel from a slight angle: aim to miss the near wire

PEELING BREAKS

It is possible for skilled players to peel a ball through more than one hoop in a break. A turn in which the last three hoops and the peg are scored for another ball is called a triple peel, and used to be the hallmark of a top player. Nowadays, a few such players are able to win a game with a sextuple: six peels in the final turn.

Yellow is being placed for a croquet stroke in which red will be peeled through the rover (last) hoop.

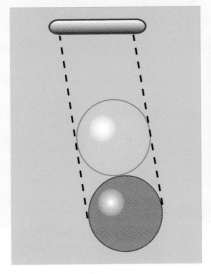

CLIPS

In Association Croquet, there is one clip for each ball, which should be placed on its next hoop at the end of a break. For the first six hoops it goes on the crown; for the second six, on the side.

ASSOCIATION CROQUET HANDICAP PLAY

Croquet has an excellent handicapping system which allows players of different abilities to play a competitive game together. The handicap takes the form of bisques, or extra turns allowed to the weaker player.

THE HANDICAP SYSTEM

Croquet Association handicaps range from –3 (for top players) to +20, but club handicaps may extend to 30 for complete beginners. The system works as follows.

1. The number of bisques received by the weaker player is the difference in the players' handicaps.

2. A half-bisque is an extra turn where no point can be scored for either side. Full bisques may not be converted into half-bisques.

3. A bisque may be taken only at the end of one of your turns. Several may be played in succession.

4. The same ball must be played in the bisque turn as was used for the previous turn.

5. Because it is a new turn, all balls become live again when a bisque is played.

6. You can only peg out your own ball if your partner ball has run all its hoops or you have pegged out an opponent's ball.

> **If you have only a few bisques, you cannot afford to spend two of them setting up a break. Instead you should be looking for opportunities to set up a four-ball break with a single bisque. In this way you will get maximum value from the bisques.**

WHEN TO TAKE A BISQUE

If you have a lot of bisques, try to use them to get a break early in the game before your expert opponent does round. In a classic opening against a scratch or minus player, for example, one or two bisques are used to set up a four-ball break. Suppose you have won the toss and put your opponent in. Your opponent has played his first ball, red, to the east boundary opposite hoop 4. You have replied by playing your first ball, blue, between his ball and the peg, announcing your intention. Your opponent may play his second ball, yellow, defensively into the second corner. You then shoot at red with black and take a bisque if you miss. This is the position shown in the diagram.

In the following stroke croquet red to hoop 2 as a pioneer with a straight drive. Black should finish close to the blue. Roquet blue, rushing it a little way towards hoop 1, and then croquet it in position as the pilot for hoop 1. Aim to play the continuation stroke to somewhere within easy distance of yellow in the second corner.

You then take a second bisque, roquet yellow and croquet it to the peg, with black finishing near red. Roquet red, take off to the pilot at hoop 1 and you have set up a perfect four-ball break with the use of two bisques.

Fig. 27: Classic opening against a scratch player: Bab has just taken a bisque (or a half-bisque) and roqueted red.

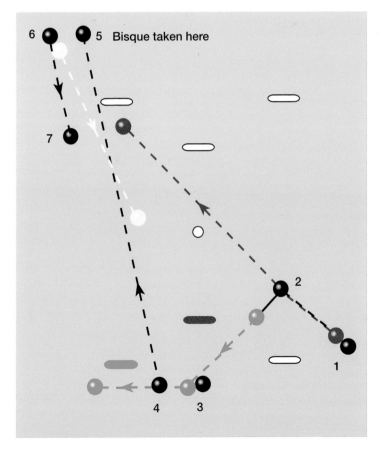

ASSOCIATION CROQUET LAWS

The full laws of Association Croquet are quite complex. However, most common situations are covered by the Basic Laws. Both can be read at http://www.croquet.org.uk, or bought as booklets from the Croquet Association Shop at the same address.

The main effects of the laws can be summarised as follows.

1. The start is from any part of either baulk-line.

2. You are entitled to a further stroke after:

(a) a roquet, after which you take croquet from the roqueted ball

(b) running your hoop, after which you play a continuation stroke

(c) a legal croquet stroke, after which you play a continuation stroke.

3. At the start of a turn or after scoring a point by running your hoop in order you may roquet and take croquet from each of the other three balls once only.

4. Your turn ends if during any stroke except a croquet stroke you neither:

(a) make a roquet; nor

(b) run your next hoop in order.

5. Your turn ends if during a croquet stroke:

(a) the croqueted ball goes off the court

(b) your ball goes off the court, unless it makes a roquet or scores its next hoop in order before leaving the court

(c) you do not move or shake the croqueted ball.

6. Your turn ends if during any stroke:

(a) you hit your ball more than once with the mallet, unless the second hit was the result of making a roquet; or

(b) you squeeze your ball between the peg or a hoop and your mallet – this is a crush stroke; or

(c) you take croquet from a ball that you were not entitled to roquet; or

(d) you play with, i.e. strike with your mallet, a wrong ball.

After faults (a) and (b), the opponent has the choice of whether or not the balls are replaced. After errors (c) and (d) all balls moved as a result are replaced in their correct positions.

7. Your turn does not end just because:

(a) you roquet a ball off the court

(b) your ball goes off the court after it has made a roquet.

8. If any balls are sent into the yard-line area (see exceptions) or off the court (no exceptions), whether or not the turn ends, they must be replaced on the yard-line opposite the point where they left court or came to rest in the yard-line area, before the next stroke. Exceptions: the striker's ball is not replaced on the yard-line if it comes to rest in the yard-line area after running its hoop in order or after a croquet stroke. In these cases the ball is played from where it lies, provided that the turn has not ended for some other reason.

9. A ball is off the court when any part of it touches or crosses the vertical plane from the inner edge of the boundary line.

10. See page 16 for when a ball has run a hoop.

11. If at the beginning of his turn a player finds that either of his balls, which has been placed where it is by his opponent, cannot hit the whole of any other ball because either a hoop or the peg is in the way or obstructs his backswing, his ball is wired. He may then lift the wired ball and play it from any position on either baulk-line.

12. A player who takes a bisque must play his bisque turn with the same ball that he was playing immediately before taking the bisque. A player who has said that he will take a bisque may change his mind before playing a stroke; but, if he indicates verbally or by quitting the court that he is not going to take a bisque, then he may not change his mind.

13. During the normal course of the game the players act as their own referees. However, if a position arises where a questionable stroke (for example a possible crush or a shot at a ball in a hoop) is about to be played, the striker should consult his opponent before playing the stroke, so that it can be specially watched. When playing a fine take-off, he must be able to say positively that he saw the croqueted ball move. Similarly, when claiming a roquet, he must be able to say positively that his ball touched the other ball.

GLOSSARY

Backswing A movement of the mallet in the opposite direction to the intended stroke.

Backward ball The ball of a side which has not made as many hoops as its partner.

Ball in hand The striker's ball when it has made a roquet.

Baulk-line The western half of the south or eastern half of the north yard-line.

Bisque An extra turn in a handicap game.

Break A turn in which more than one point is scored.

Break down To make a mistake so that your turn comes to an end involuntarily during a break.

Casting Repeatedly swinging the mallet over the ball while preparing to hit it.

Continuation stroke An extra stroke earned after scoring a hoop or playing a croquet stroke.

Corner spots Where the yard-line has a right-angle in it.

Croquet stroke To strike your ball which has been placed in contact with the ball it roqueted, so that they both move.

Croqueted ball The ball from which croquet has been taken.

Drive A natural croquet stroke played with normal follow-through.

Forward ball The ball of a side which has made more hoops than the other.

Free shot An opportunity to shoot at a ball or balls which gives no advantage to the opponent if the shot is missed.

Full roll A roll stroke in which the balls go the same distance.

Half-roll A roll stroke in which the croqueted ball goes twice as far as the striker's ball.

Hit in To make a roquet when you are the out-player.

Hoop approach A croquet stroke with the aim of getting the striker's ball in position to run the hoop in the continuation stroke.

In-player The player who has the innings and thereby the advantage.

Laying up Deliberately ending a turn, in the hope of scoring hoops in your next turn after your opponent has missed.

Lift To lift your ball from where it lies and play it from a baulk-line.

Out-player The player without the innings.

Peel To send a ball other than your own through its next hoop in order.

Peg out To make a rover ball hit the peg and thus be removed from the game.

Penalty spots The points half-way up the west and east boundaries where balls that have prematurely advanced to the next hoop are placed.

Penult The penultimate hoop or the last hoop but one.

Pilot ball The ball off which you make a hoop.

Pioneer ball The ball which is waiting at your next hoop but one.

Pivot ball The auxiliary ball in a four-ball break.

Roll A croquet stroke played in such a way as to increase the distance travelled by the striker's ball relative to the croqueted ball.

Roquet To make your ball hit another.

Rover A ball which has made all its hoops and may be pegged out or may peg out other rovers. Also, the last hoop.

Rover peel Scoring the last hoop for a ball other than the striker's ball.

Running the hoop Scoring a hoop point by causing a ball to pass through its hoop in order, in the correct direction.

Rush To roquet a ball to a predetermined position.

Split A croquet stroke in which the balls go in different directions.

Stalking Walking along the line of aim to position the body before playing a stroke.

Stop shot A croquet stroke played in such a way as to decrease the distance travelled by the striker's ball relative to the croqueted ball.

Take off A croquet stroke which sends the striker's ball to a predetermined position and moves the croqueted ball by a relatively small amount.

Tice A ball played to a position, usually from a baulk-line, which is intended to entice the opponent to shoot at it.

Wired A ball is wired if a hoop or the peg obscures the direct line of the striker's ball to any part of it or if a hoop or the peg interferes with the normal swing of the mallet.

Yard-line An imaginary line 1 yard in from the boundary.

Yard-line area The area between the yard-line and the boundary.

INDEX